The Burning Green

BY

JOHN AND NANCY MCKENNA

Resource *Publications*

An imprint of *Wipf and Stock Publishers*
199 West 8th Avenue • Eugene OR 97401

Resource *Publications*
an imprint of Wipf and Stock Publishers
150 West Broadway
Eugene, Oregon 97401

The Burning Green
By McKenna, John and McKenna, Nancy
©1996 McKenna, John and McKenna, Nancy
ISBN: 0-9653517-1-8
Publication Date: August, 1996
Previously published by , 1996.

The Burning Green

TABLE OF CONTENTS

fOREWORÒ

Our poetry expresses the person we are as man and woman, husband and wife together. Throughout our more than twenty years of marriage, Nancy and I have struggled to give these poems a voice that might reflect the gift of God with us.

We are of a time that is deeply wounded. Our language echos its rage and folly. We are thankful to be free from its destructive power. To this freedom we hope our poems will point their readers. The Bible verses are meant to help us hear.

John and Nancy McKenna
Pasadena, California
Spring, 1996

iv

THE BURNING GREEN POEMS

The Burning Green

To give to dreams a flesh
Is not matter man can tailor
But skin from the terrors of wild things.
Like animals from fire
Flee the burning green,
We scream for land to mantle
The nakedness we wear,
The dark upon our fears.

Now you must go with me
And gaze upon this country
But blazing eyes can bear,
God clothe with light his lovers
And dress from earth his care.

For we know that if the earthly tent we live in is destroyed, we have a building from God, a house not made with hands, eternal in the heavens. Here indeed we groan, and long to put on our heavenly dwelling, so that by putting it on we may not be found naked. For while we are still in this tent, we sigh with anxiety; not that we would be unclothed, but that we would be further clothed, so that what is mortal may be swallowed up by life. He who has prepared us for this very thing is God, who has given us the Spirit as a guarantee. So we are always of good courage; we know that while we are at home in the body we are away from the Lord, for we walk by faith, not by sight. We are of good courage, and we would rather be away from the body and at home with the Lord. So whether we are at home or away, we make it our aim to please him.

2 Cor 5:1-9

CHRIST CHILD

Like the seas change
Land and the longing
Dark wraps like arms
The earth in sound,
A small child pushes in his hand
His dreams into a blue sky.

And round the beginningless roar
He alone who reigns holily
Shall take and hold,
For as long as forever is,
Their flesh in His.

Now therefore, O kings, be wise; be warned, O rulers of the earth. Serve the Lord with fear, with trembling kiss his feet, lest he be angry, and you perish in the way; for his wrath is quickly kindled. Blessed are all who take refuge in him.

Psalms 2:10-12

5

The Loudest of Kings

Almost without sound,
For all the noise in the world,
Our lives would praise
The loudest of kings.
The winds of our time,
Burning the rightness of our clocks,
Tell through the withering trees
It is the thunder of crying
That crashes down our streets.
It is a cacophony of dying.
It is the hermetics of sin
Gnaws the metal of our age,
The insect that hears a robot's thought.
Empty, as a symbol is without him,
It is upon the hill
His cross
Stands still over the roar about us,
And secret as a center
It is his life that moves
All who must go to him.
Quiet as an atom bursts
And quick as the watchers look
He alone has words for it.
Almost without sound,
For all the noise in the world,
Our lives would praise
The loudest of kings.

He will swallow up death for ever, and the Lord God will wipe away tears from all faces, and the reproach of his people he will take away from all the earth; for the Lord has spoken. It will be said on that day, "Lo, this is our God; we have waited for him, that he might save us. This is the Lord; we have waited for him; let us be glad and rejoice in his salvation."

Isaiah 25: 8-9

The hour

The smooth sun rises
And moonlight slips like a dream
Out where stars age softly on
Time's turning love.
The hour dawns upon the table
Hard as weeping
And the slow sad ruin of the world
Wears down to a whisper
A breaking that is not bone.
Yet this is not the good breaking.
Like the sea pounds the land,
Like lightening knifed the dark
Still thundering in his eyes,
Battered man and moment meet
By the wound of forever
The cross that cuts the veil,
That death and joy shall hear
In the loudest kind of light
Man was made for waking.

8

Therefore it is said, "Awake, O sleeper, and arise from the dead, and Christ shall give you light."

Ephesians 5:14

shells

Upon the wounded sea,
Home in their kiss,
Time and wind bring
In the ways of water
Lovers swept upon the shores;
Upon the still sand,
Where faded sea shells roar,
Long ago broken
They break once more.
In the sound of stars
Lips shape to tell
In the rush of words
Together upon another,
Crashing in their mouths
Their nearly crushed need.
He comes alone who listens,
An ancient tear upon his face.
Shall we sound
And hear his name?

If any of you lacks wisdom, let him ask God, who gives to all men generously and without reproaching, and it will be given him. But let him ask in faith, with no doubting, for he who doubts is like a wave of the sea that is driven and tossed by the wind.

James 1: 5-6

ANOTHER DEATH

A meteor of my mother's pain,
I unable to begin
In my heedless rage
Mad with emptiness
And the dread of nothingness
Was flung alive onto my hollow age,
Bitter upon my kind's abyss.
There I would hunt
Wherever I found them
Dark shapes of women
Falling in the long night,
Like the waves of their hair,
Thundering in our dying years,
When we would roll over
The bones of our fathers.
It was always goodby then,
Goodby forever,
When we paid with our flesh
The still longer desire.
It was always goodby,
Goodby forever.
Here the breathless creatures
Crouch like clouds in a black sky,
Shape for the storm the kill
That screams in a red rain
That beats upon our hearts,
Who gasp while reaching out
At last to die.
Hear now my primordial cry,
That he who made you made me
With another death than our own
To sign the sound the deaf hear first,
That Christ aloud with His Spirit takes
A beginningless man from his tomb.

I acknowledged my sin to thee, and I did not hide my iniquity; I said, "I will confess my transgressions to the Lord"; then thou didst forgive the guilt of my sin. Selah

Psalms 32:5

the Longing

May my mortal long
With mortal longing
Always for his beginning.
May my selves, the dying,
Follow like a star
His seed to birth,
That in the grip of death and love
He who tells what seed may bear
Shall flower in the sun for me,
Or all my mortal longing be
But for the longing dead.

Through him then let us continually offer up a sacrifice of praise to God, that is, the fruit of lips that acknowledge his name.

Hebrews 13:15

The Last Look

Not alone their first love,
When eyes are strong
And there echos mortally
The eternity of their kiss,
Would they crush with their bliss
The first worm of the world alive
In the arms of the whirling winds,
When the tacit rush with death
Doomed a dread race's embrace.
Agony is an ancient wound then,
A cut in the quick of their eyes,
A blow on the beat of their hearts,
Who must know in beginning
Or see with their ruin
Time itself astonished.
Where once the stars
Easy in the night sky
Whispered on the dark
The forever they touched
And the secret of their miracles
Moved by the oil of their eyes
Across the sceptre of their rainbows,
The clouds blazing in the hour
Aging on the light's abyss,
They held longingly flame and fire
To slip shapelessly down
Onto the sleep of the earth:
And this shall be the last look---
The living holy one called!

They will pass through the land, greatly distressed and hungry; and when they are hungry, they will be enraged and will curse their king and their God, and turn their faces upward; and they will look to the earth, but behold, distress and darkness, the gloom of anquish; and they will be thrust into thick darkness.

Isaiah 8:21-22

BETTER KNOWN

Bent on the blows this vanishing world
Made of the muscle of my heart,
I am more fearless now than the boy
Running with his eyes shut
In the pain of his nothingness
Over the lonely hours of a scream
Echoing down a terror's abyss
To a hag at the center of the world.
Nor will time ever be again
Some posture of a crux for me,
The gasp of our tears
Or the loveless grip
That seasons our years to write
The calendar of our days
Under the sun, under the stars.
It will never be like that again.

I am more fearless than the boy
Now that I am better known.

For God did not give us a spirit of timidity but a spirit of power and love and self-control.

2 Timothy 1:7

fLASbING fACE

Over the green hills
The wild horse runs
With flashing face,
Galloping like the sun
Upon the warm earth.
Who spurs this strength
As clouds would stride
The windswept sky
Until among the stars
Wide open as the moon
His eyes would gaze,
No words I know can tell.
Yet a great magnificence
Moves across the ages,
Where we are made to glimpse
The way his love has gone.

Did you give the horse might? Do you clothe his neck with strength? Do you make him leap like the locust? His majestic snorting is terrible. He paws in the valley, and exults in his strength; he goes out to meet the weapons.

Job 39:19-21

WEIGHT BY LIGHT

Weight by light
The waters of the world,
The weathers of an age
The fish shall swim
And do not tell the winds
The shape a home shall take
And do not dare to say
They are the same,
Fish and water,
Wind and man.
Light by light is light,
Hours are shaped to fame
The distances of clocks
No lottery can run.
What chance is there
The fish shall swim aloud
Or man upon the spinning earth
Breathe a word to bear
The promise of this holy love?
It is a promise
Only God shall keep.

The true light that enlightens every man was coming into the world. He was in the world, and the world was made through him, yet the world knew him not.

John 1:9-10

The Long Night

...for Tommy McKenna

As starlight grows the distance
The moon glows softly on
And the lost light of day
Slips alive upon his face,
In the vastness of the long night
He gazes in his rage and emptiness
(Most men live by their manias!)
Out over the tormented hours.
He listens tearlessly
As the loveless grip of the world
Grasps his terror in its sound,
From which we hide our sighs,
Howling in our life's abyss
Among the ruin of his race.
We do not mourn as loudly
As our longing truly is.
We do not make prayers like screams,
When God has knelt to take us
To Himself.

I am praying for them; I am not praying for the world but for those whom thou hast given me, for they are thine; all mine are thine, and thine are mine, and I am glorified in them.

John 17:9-10

the call

...for the artist, Francis Bacon

Hands holding the silence
In the motion of a room,
Light left long ago deafened
In the spaces of the dark,
An ancient kill
Telling time embraced by lions
Myths imaged in a moment
Impassable as stone,
As if we were here now
To vanish into nothingness,
Something that has never been,
Something that should never be
Or soon will never be again,
The crux of a primordial scream
Mocking the great I-AM.

Wither shall I go from thy Spirit? Or wither shall I flee from thy Presence?

Psalms 139:7

The Blood Strong Day

Dark is a way we wake,
The clocks by torment
Ticking upon the great earth,
The hours of an age
Limping through its light's abyss,
Held in the pitiless grip.
Dark is a long way then,
The woman of the city,
A rose in the rain,
Suffocating with phantoms
The machinations of men,
Who crush into a groan
Their love among the thorns.
Dark is a long way then,
The smell of tears
Sounding upon the floor,
Their thundering through the streets,
When the hour sails
And the ghost-wind wounds.
Still the light shall sing
The blood strong day aloud.

When morning came, all the chief priests and the elders of the people took counsel against Jesus to put him to death; and they bound him and led him away and delivered him to Pilate the governor.

Matthew 27: 1-2

The Forgiven

Among the thundering,
When lightening strikes
And the whisper of the stars
Breaks across the summer sky,
The blazing clouds storm
The stones with this light's blood,
When the winds of time wash clean
The weather of our eyes
And the ghosts we have known
And the dark about us here
Flee like a groan away,
And among our wounds
We hear what only the forgiven see.

When I saw him, I fell at his feet as though dead. But he laid his right hand upon me, saying, "Fear not, I am the first and the last, and the living one; I died, and behold I am alive for evermore, and I have the keys of Death and Hades.

Revelation 1:17-18

COVERED BY MOONLIGHT

---for a poet laureate of
Great Britain, Jack Clemo

Along the rugged healing sea,
With seabirds and hills
At home in the sky,
Covered by moonlight,
He walks as a stone
Numb to numbering
With night sounds, stars,
And the tears he has known.
His hands,
Like crabs along the shore,
See with blind eyes
The voice of waters,
Hear with deaf ears
The burning of holy love,
And he knows sleeplessly
The one who goes there
In the full fury, sight, and thunder,
As from a dream his wife
Meteors with her sudden flesh,
Covered by moonlight,
Their kiss in the shadow of his death.
Always along the sands
Slowly a tide is rising,
The waters wearing
Against rock and lovers
The prayers of his bare hands,
Covered by moonlight.

Moreover the light of the moon will be as the light of the sun, and the light of the sun will be sevenfold, as the light of seven days, in the day when the Lord binds up the hurt of his people, and heals the wounds inflicted by his blow.

Isaiah 30:26

The Astonished Silence

He stands and sings,
A peculiar figure of a man,
Some say crazed,
Of Christ and his cross to the crowd,
Beneath tall buildings
That cavern this corner of the city.
They mock him and they laugh,
They name him names,
Like Adam with animals,
And like jaguars slip away
For comfort with the pack.
When he is gone,
Within the astonished silence,
I watched the desolation grow.

I walk before the Lord in the land of the living. I kept my faith, even when I said, "I am greatly afflicted," I said in my consternation, "Men are all a vain hope."

Psalms 116:9-11

the Last of Light and sleep

Death on the streets of a city
Is a bitter end for an old man
Covered by the rags of his age
And a rage no one could bear.
His eyes, coal black and cold,
Watched the madness in the skies,
The sea-birds cawing among the clouds,
Heard the sound above the grave hills,
Grey as the hairs of his skull,
Lost in the lashing of his bones.
Turned to stone, his need
Bore the metal of his days
Melt in a sun but minutes away,
His rotted love almost gone.
No matter what he has denied,
Waiting for the last of light and sleep,
May the cross he wrapped about his neck,
Bear in the crack of his dreams,
Before he wakes or not,
Christ's quickening blood,
And the eye of his soul rest.

What shall I render to the Lord for all his bounty to me? I will lift up the cup of salvation and call on the name of the Lord, I will pay my vows to the Lord in the presence of his people. Precious in the sight of the Lord is the death of his saints.

Psalms 116:12-15

Love Let to the Bone

Love let to the bone
Evil cut a wound,
Words in the wind
Sound a sea of tears
Falling on the floor.
The weeping of the tides,
Like the gift of gab,
Waters a heart bloodless,
Sails the race to shed
On the horizon of its sleep
The brutes of love,
Vows to print time's hunger
Upon the smooth sand.
The fish upon the table
Sees the sacred kiss
Sip the desire of the world
In the nick of time.
Love let to the bone
Evil cut a wound.

"Behold, the days are coming," says the Lord God, "when I will send a famine on the land; not a famine of bread, nor a thirst for water, but of hearing the words of the Lord. They shall wander from sea to sea, and from north to east; they shall run to and fro, to seek the word of the Lord, but they shall not find it."

Amos 8:11-12

A DESERT WORLD

Now in my burning days,
When the primordial dumbness
Desolates the words of my kind
And makes our world a desert,
With my hair a flame,
Conquered,
I stand on the searing sands
And call in the whirling winds.
I would sound so always
The unconsummable fire might fire
To make a future yours,
That all the mad or thankless ages,
Shimmering like mirages,
Might vanish before your gaze,
That all the screamful centuries,
Asleep in the sun,
Might rage no more
Across our ancient wound.
Though the skull to sight,
In the multitudes of tears
In the skies of praise
In the blazing clouds,
I would his holy hour come,
That the conflagration of his cross
Write with his fiery peace
Your name in his blood,
And all the pages of forever cry
What only his forgiven love.

I came to cast fire upon the earth; and would that it were already kindled!

Luke 12: 49

ONE TEAR IS ENOUGH

One tear is enough.
A whole century of thought
Might worm a way to say
This is enough, my love,
The whole passion of an age
Roll into tears
All its dry years.
But we are cactus, my love,
Watered in a desert,
The nightly bloom in a sandy hour
When the quiet moon whispers
The secret among the stars,
A flower for morning dew,
When the great fashions of clocks,
Indifferent to our need,
Timed away on a roar
Far from the wasteland
Filling our season.
We should call ourselves rosebuds,
Snowflakes, or molten things,
Were it not for his cross.
Without it,
No one would call us Man.
The hour has come.
One tear is enough.

When Jesus had spoken these words, he lifted up his eyes to heaven and said, "Father, the hour has come; glorify thy Son that the Son may glorify thee, since thou hast given him power over all flesh, to give eternal life to all who thou hast given him. And this is eternal life, that they know thee the only true God, and Jesus Christ whom thou has sent."

John 17:1-3

43

GENTLE heIRARChIES

---for W. Jim Neidhardt,
Quantum Physicist

Without the Word of God
How can we hear stars,
Listen for the moon,
Or love light a way
To a home for our thought?
For with these sounds
Fish remember,
The earth sings,
And the gentle heirarchies
Lift a child to the passion
Telling the humble to see
The flowering of the Light.

If the Lord had not been my help, my soul would soon have dwelt in the land of silence.

Psalms 94:17

ТЬЕ FACE

Where no heart is
The time of light
Oils an image of the hour,
The meaning of a wound,
Where no eye can touch
The shape of things to come.
Upon the retina of a kiss
The secret in the hand holds
The moving of the world.
No tears shape the moment
We see the deathless face.

For now we see in a mirror dimly, but then face to face. Now I know in part; then I shall understand fully, even as I have been fully understood.

1 Corinthians 13:12

ÐANGER IS BEST

For those who have been prepared,
Danger is best.
Do not fear, my friend,
Be strong and endure.
We shall know best
How then we shall live.
Let the moon by night
And the sun by day
Say to the enemy
Time is a sacred place,
Made with a rest
The only God gives.
Do not fear, my friend,
Be strong and endure.

Be watchful, stand firm in your faith, be courageous, be strong. Let all that you do be done in love.

1 Corinthians 16:13-14

MADE TO WONDER

The voice upon the mountains
With holy thunder
Tells the lightening of his presence.
It is more perfect than we know,
Who are made to wonder.

There are many voices
Echoing on the floor
Like the pictures on the walls
Speaking to each other,
Or no one there at all.

In the silence of the room
It was not her who entered
Or never came at all.
It was not her at all.

The voice upon the mountains
Is more perfect than we know,
Who are made to wonder.

For the Lord God of Hosts has a day of tumult and trampling and confusion in the valley of vision, a battering down of walls and a shouting to the mountains.

Isaiah 22:5

51

ƒAKING IT

There is in eternity,
I believe,
Too much passion for you.
That is why your smile
Only ever reminds me
Of your teeth.

Crush a fool in a mortar with a pestle along with crushed grain, yet his folly will not depart from him.

Proverbs 27:22

WHERE NO TIME LOOKS

Even if a man on the moon walks,
He would not find the matter
A generation must mirror.
In a fearless step
Beyond the holy dark
Where no time looks
The oil of his might smiles
Upon the face of our frail flesh
And in the places we have gone,
The horror we have known,
The hour of his tear sounds.

In the days of his flesh, Jesus offered up prayers and supplications, with loud cries and tears, to him who was able to save him from death, and he was heard for his godly fear.

Hebrews 5:7

The Deathless Light

...for Tom Torrance

Even though I once heard
The rumors of the grave,
Dusts blown wildly aloud
Across the howling chasm,
Mirrored by a thousand passions,
Haunting our gaze,
The eloquence of your voice
Shaped the deathless light for me
In the secrets of my room.
Now among the listeners,
I have heard you say
He comes to carry us across
Through the real fire.

While he carries me,
I will thank him for you there.

He who reaps receives wages, and gathers fruit for eternal life, so that sower and reaper may rejoice together.

John 4:36

HERE NOW MY SLUMBER ENDS

...for my wife, Nancy

Here now my slumber ends,
Who must wake so horrified;
How tell a man his heart
Whose heart is torn with rage?
Better a lovely woman there,
Of skin as white as moon,
Than the howling of his age.
Warm and brave she is
Whom I shall love
Before me,
Who has known his bitter cage.

This I command you, to love one another.

John 15:17

ROJA

It was a flame,
Her hair in the wind
A ruby dancing in the sun,
Her blue eyes like the sky,
Oiling with her smile
The distances of stars
In the secret of her face,
Like Adam's rib,
Amazing the world for me.

Strength and dignity are her clothing, and she laughs at the time to come.

Proverbs 31:25

The Cactus

In the lonesome desert,
Cooled beneath the moon's long shadow,
The cactus keeps the promised flower
For the face of God.

Lord, hear my prayer!

I love the Lord, because he has heard my voice and my supplications, because he inclined his ear to me, therefore I will call on him as long as I live.

Psalms 116:1-2

WHENEVER I REMEMBER

Whenever I remember
The cool and coal black face,
The metal of the Irish race,
You used to gaze upon a boy,
The tough and tearless twist
Turned into a fist of dreams
Of your rough love,
I cry, my father.

Yet we could hear the grasses grow!

You struck
With such fierce force
A child's wrong and ear
And with your brokenness and fear
You crushed my nothingness and tears,
As if a thought,
Something you had been taught
Was law enough
For the lightening of my song.

Yet we could hear the grasses grow!

And I learned too
Your lonesomeness on earth,
Warping the ecstasy of time for me,
The empty bottle in the stall,
Deceitful kiss,
Sexual spasm,
And the liquors of the long nights
Not even a next day could end.

Yet we could hear the grasses grow!

So it was the thunder of steel
Across her living screeching room,
Your wife, my mother, stitching
The tapestry of our lives
With memories like wounds

On the scars of your graves,
Two stones that God has heard
Cut to the sounds of war.

Yet we could hear the grasses grow!

You know that you were ransomed from the futile ways inherited from your fathers, not with perishable things such as silver or gold, but with the precious blood of Christ, like that of a lamb without blemish or spot.

1 Peter 1:18-19

The Eagle's Song

The eagle rides the winds
Silent in the heavens
And below the damp earth sleeps
In the smell of rain and roses,
When death reads the stones
Carved above their graves.
With the breath of God
They hear the eagle's song.

I wait for the Lord, my soul waits, and in his word I hope; my soul waits for the Lord more than the watchmen for the morning, more than the watchmen for the morning.

Psalms 130:5-6

the passion

A crossless justice like a ghost
Haunts the famine in the land
And moral indignation as a voice
Shrouds the earth in desolation.
He devestates the promise of the world
Who calls man against man again,
And makes the freedom of our kind
A peacock strutting.
He devours the need of the blind
And God alive or not
Would take his maker captive
And pervert what is to come.
What is to come?
Rough beast or phantom,
Christ has said he will.

Behold, I am coming soon, bringing my recompense, to repay every one for what he has done. I am the Alpha and the Omega, the First and the Last, the Beginning and the End.

Revelation 22:12-13

THE GHETTO

It is not so much the thing itself,
But that we can pretend
We are not in it.

As in water face answers face, so the mind of man reflects the man.

Proverbs 27:19

INTERCESSION

"We fear, we fear. Who shall plead for me,
Who intercede for me, in my most need?"

...T.S. Eliot, <u>Murder in the</u>
<u>Cathedral</u>

We have gone out,
You and I,
And we have gazed.
We have seen the abyss.
We did not stay in backyards,
Sit and stare,
After we had heard the laughter there,
After we had heard the sound of glass.
We knew we could break.
We have gone out,
You and I,
And we have gazed.
We have seen the abyss.

We will not speak of it,
No, we shall not speak of it,
We cannot speak of it.
It is an unspeakable thing.
But for the screams,
Our endless echos there,
There is no sound from it.
Like the dark in the depths of the seas,
A deeper dark than darkness
Darkens the depths of our dread.
We will not speak of it.

Hear us, holy Father, then.

Do not be afraid of sudden panic, or of the ruin of the wicked, when it comes; for the Lord will be your confidence and will keep your foot from being caught.

Proverbs 3:25-26

Tbe VICTOR'S SONG

When beginning is begun,
The enemy falls
And out of the ruins
The victor's song sung.
The whispers of stars
Shine with quiet beauty
In the secret night.
The earth is quaked aloud
And the torments of the age
Howl for the listener.
The child sobs alive
In the din of war.
Like thunder in a sky,
He comes to lift up to his bosom
The small smooth face,
To keep like the moon
His sabbath there.
When beginning is begun,
The enemy falls
And out of the ruins
The victor's song sung.

The Lord, your God, is in your midst, a warrior who gives victory; he will rejoice over you with gladness, he will renew you in his love; he will exult over you with loud singing as on a day of festival.

Zephaniah 3:17

The Bloody Years

Time tormented hours
Wooed away from ruin
The groan of our kiss,
When flesh we needed most
Weighed down our arms
And fears imagined or not
Seemed always on the horizon,
When we learned of love,
my love.

Bearing the wounds of a generation
We wept to cross,
We made our dreams
Cover like an aether
The bed of our laughter there,
When we raged to remember
What no one knew,
When we learned of love,
my love.

When we learned of love,
Angel blessed,
The spinning world
Left time unspoken
Wrecked on the bloody years,
Where Christ gave bone and muscle
And we learned of love,
my love.

Show us thy steadfast love, O Lord, and grant us thy salvation.

Psalms 85:7

keepinG WatcH

...for Margaret & Emory McKenna

He climbs the stairs once more,
Enters the coldness of her room,
And sits another evening
In the darkness beside her,
Keeping watch.

The woman
With her nightmares
Lies dying on their bed.
What she has been,
What she is no longer,
Lives inside him there.
Keeping watch,
He sees her
As no man ever will.

Three things are too wonderful for me; four I do not understand: the way of an eagle in the sky, the way of a serpent on a rock, the way of a ship on the high seas, and the way of a man with a maiden.

Proverbs 30:18-19

THE ECCENTRIC

They thought him eccentric.
He saw in the ransom
The secret of the center.
The gaze they demanded
He refused to pay.
He thought his friend
Was God Himself.

And he said to them, "To you has been given the secret of the kingdom of God, but for those outside everything is in parables."

Mark 4:11

mouths wide open

The hour shapes into a home
The wilderness we bore,
Nerves hanging on the walls,
Hunger longing like the worm
Beneath the nails of our hands.
What we were then
Embraced the emptiness
Burning time itself
Down an age's fiery blast,
As if the primordial wounding knifed us
And we could only limp in silence
On the desert of our rooms.
As light sounds lightening
We held together
The days tuned aloud
To the ticking of clocks
And the metal of the sky
Came ringing at the door
And the spell of molten things
Melted into ash
The vows that murdered murder.

With our mouths wide open,
We are made to listen.

Besides this you know what hour it is, how it is full time now for you to wake from sleep. For salvation is nearer to us now than when we first believed; the night is far gone, the day is at hand. Let us then cast off the works of darkness and put on the armor of light.

Romans 13:11-12

The Vastness of The Glass

In the silence of the long night,
As if he were not truly there,
He deafly cracked against escape
The doom of an exitless thought
And wrote with his blood
A word for his death.
(I remember the picture:
The nude body of a man
Slumped at the bottom of a bottle,
Its cork his head,
His severed nerves
Falling like lightening
Down the empty hours.
He held in his hand the lily,
His face screaming from above
Out the vastness of the glass.)
In the darkness unalone
The voice that triumphs on the cross
Must have been the laughter there.
I cannot picture it for you.
When God has spoken,
What can a picture do?

Thou hast kept count of my tossings; put thou my tears in thy bottle! Are they not in thy book?

Psalms 56:8

THE BLOOD OF LIGHT

The blood of light
Pierces the eyes
In the retina of the dead,
The dumbness of our time.
The creatures of the deep,
Weathering our knowing,
Swarm like locusts on waves of war,
Sounding for a fear's breath
To fuse the seeking of our screams
In the chasm of the world.
Yet unforsaken
He slashes into a path
The darkness we have known,
The dust we have been.
Death is
Never the last word.

So Jesus said to them, "Truly, truly, I say to you, unless you eat the flesh of the Son of man and drink his blood, you have no life in you; he who eats my flesh and drinks my blood has eternal life, and I will raise him up at the last day."

John 6:53-54

EMBRACED BY STARLIGHT

...for Boris Kuharetz,
Astrophysicist

Famous as the sun,
The caverns of the city,
When the skyscrapers race
To impale their gods
And reach to rip apart a sky
And heaven with our rage
The shape of their power,
Bear as a child looks
The city's knifely dread
Onto the bosom of its mother,
And easy as moonlight is,
Lovers in the lonely park,
Past pools of shaded waters,
Cool green trees that shadow,
Like a woman remembered,
The woods in the rain,
Horse drawn couples
Clopping through warm smells
That summer the homeless there,
Embraced by starlight,
He moves invisibly
As a man is able
To his locker-room in the world.
"It must be music,
Or it is not real," he whispers,
His voice surprising in the air,
Remembering the violin
His father once played,
Unopened in its case now
For fear of the neighbors,
Lost among the chaos of thieves.
The taxi driver does not hear
Anything but a name,
And in the metal of his time
In the silence of the room,
Embraced by starlight,

He lies down upon his bed
To sleep, like the bow
His fingers had known
Held in the tauntness of strings
Singing on the shapely wood
The dance of his memories.
"It must be music,
Or it is not real," he says,
The stars lighting on the walls
The longing of his love
In the rolling of his dreams.
When he wakes,
He crosses the room,
Stands beside the window
To gaze out over the muffled sounds
The caverns of the city
Make beneath his blazing eyes,
And then closes them to pray,
Embraced by starlight.

The secret things belong to the Lord God; but the things that are revealed belong to us and to our children forever, that we may do all the words of this law.

Deuteronomy 29:29

KRYSTAL-NACHT

The sacred day seasons
A fearless moment for us,
Gives our land its light
And tells of things to come.
Cracked across a centerless world
Shattered on a sea of stars,
Broken dreams,
Broken rocks,
Broken glass,
And the black back of days
Are told by the Krystal-Nacht of time
The holy dawn is rising.
Watch, my love,
Brokenness is not forever.

I hear, and my body trembles, my lips quiver at the sound; rottenness enters into my bones, my steps totter beneath me. I will quietly wait for the day of trouble to come upon people who invade us.

Habakkuk 3:16

The FLOWERS OF THE FIELD

Not the proud man apart,
Mastering with an eye
The powers of the spinning world,
His vision shimmering on the skies,
Nor the great woman,
The longed for beauty
Straight as the light of day,
With her shapely strength
Like a statue in the park,
Not even the most patriot,
His determined face
Turned in a sacred gaze
Above the howling throngs
Like clouds blazing in a sun,
But the terrible children,
Their screams in the dark,
The flowers of the field
Green as the abyss is dumb,
Exploded like meteors
Into the dread shapes that torment
The aching of our memory,
Who heard with animal eyes
Like ghosts in the silence
The stallion standing on the hill
Under the moon's nightly ride.
Across the grief of all the years
The bell tolls; be not afraid.
Listen: This is my body
Given for you,
Take and eat.
Listen: This is my cup,
Given for you,
Take and drink.
Do this in remembrance of me,
For I remember for you.

I have said all this to you to keep you from falling away. They will put you out of the synagogues; indeed, the hour is coming when whoever kills you will think he is offering service to God. And they will do this because they have not known the Father, nor me. But I have said these things to you, that when their hour comes you may remember that I told you of them.

John 16:1-4

IN THE WILDERNESS OF THEIR SONGS

...for Michael & Alex Smith

Years and years of heartbeats wear,
Seasons by time remembered,
The green truths of love's passions.
They glimpsed with their lives,
Tasted the measure of fruits lost,
The meaning of their cries,
Always unknown and fleeting.
Bearing it all broke the boys
In the wilderness of their songs.
How can we number their tears
Writing on the wall their wounds,
The thing no one can remember,
When the boys ran with their eyes shut
Over the fields of their pain?
Down the dank dark stench
Where no one is ever held
Our age's machine slips,
Wombed with a deadly kiss.
Touching the shame that carved
The light from their eyes,
Their faces watered the lonely lake,
Watching the grip of their mother's guilt.
To what have we been sentenced?
Now in the midnight of a moonrise
Upon the sands along the shore,
A footfall for a little monument
Prints their tale upon the ages,
And I do not know if there is time
To tell it all or why,
Time to remind ourselves once more
Before we say another word
Of their question in the sky.
With the vanishing of their tears
And never numbered tone of them
We need to know the logic of their longing
Over the picture on their grave.
Bearing it all broke the boys
In the wilderness of their songs.

He reached from on high, he took me, he drew me out of many waters. He delivered me from my strong enemy, from those who hated me; for they were too mighty for me. They came upon me in the day of my calamity; but the Lord was my stay.

2 Samuel 22:17-19

THE SWAN IN WINTER

Upon the quiet snow,
Shaping the barren silences,
The swan in winter hears
The coolness of the starlight's distances
Blanketed above the moon.
In this season of the world,
She waits to speak of things
Only her longing can tell,
As if her wings were wed
To a memory lost long ago,
Her forgotten flight
And the wonder of her beauty
Filling like a tear the heavens.

Surely there is a future, and your hope will not be cut off.

Proverbs 23:18

tbe impossible sigNificaNce

Is where I stand
A place no one has been?
Is where I must listen,
Haunted by my nothingness,
The place I hear?
In the torment of my scream's abyss
I have long been ravaged,
Gone with many on a rage
For which the graves are famous,
Telling us death is alive.
Yet he is good,
Heals my strange escape
With the holiness of his love,
Of which I hardly ever speak.
It is fearsome to learn
There is a boundary
Being made that hears
This love shape time,
Love as solid as the truth
Who names a thing for me
And carries me across the deep
To the impossible significance.

Since therefore the children share in flesh and blood, he himself likewise partook of the same nature, that through death he might destroy him who has the power of death, that is the devil, and deliver all those who through fear of death were subject to lifelong bondage.

Hebrews 2:14-15

IF YOU ARE LAZARUS

If you are Lazarus
And the universe is your tomb,
Body, time, and space
Your mummy clothes,
And your heart a slab of stone,
As love heals the dead
The light shall hurt your eyes.
For we are made of dust and nothingness
By the breath of God
A little less than Him,
Made to hear and know His Word
Or without Him to pretend.
Love does not live for death
And neither shall Man.
When the stone is moved,
You will hear Him call.

Truly, truly, I say to you, unless a grain of wheat falls into the earth and dies, it remains alone; but if it dies, it bears much fruit. He who loves his life loses it, and he who hates his life in this world will keep it for eternal life.

John 12:24-25